The My Encyclopedia Collection

My Encyclopedia of Baby Animals
My Encyclopedia of the Forest
My Encyclopedia of Insects and Bugs
My Encyclopedia of the Sea

Library of Congress Cataloging-in-Publication Data

Names: Louisy, Patrick, author. | Axelson, Joy Nevin, translator.
Title: My encyclopedia of the sea / Patrick Louisy ; translated by Joy Nevin Axelson.
Other titles: Mon encyclo de la mer. English
Description: New York, NY : Children's Press, an imprint of Scholastic, Inc., [2017] | Series: My encyclopedia
Identifiers: LCCN 2016008900| ISBN 9780531224731 (library binding) | ISBN 9780531225974 (hardcover)
Subjects: LCSH: Oceanography–Juvenile literature. | Oceanography–Encyclopedias, Juvenile. | Marine ecology–Juvenile literature. | Marine ecology–Encyclopedias, Juvenile. | Marine animals–Juvenile literature. | Marine animals–Encyclopedias, Juvenile. | Marine plants–Juvenile literature. | Marine plants-Encyclopedias, Juvenile.
Classification: LCC QH541.5.S3 L6813 2017 | DDC 577.7–dc23 LC record available at http://lccn.loc.gov/2016008900

Produced by Spooky Cheetah Press
Translation by Joy Nevin Axelson

Printed in China 62

1 2 3 4 5 6 7 8 9 10 R 25 24 23 22 21 20 19 18 17 16

My encyclopedia of the sea

Patrick Louisy

Table of Contents

page 67

Who Lives Under the Sea?

page 79

Return to the Sea

page 87

Attack and Defense

page 105

Social Life

page 115

Underwater Babies

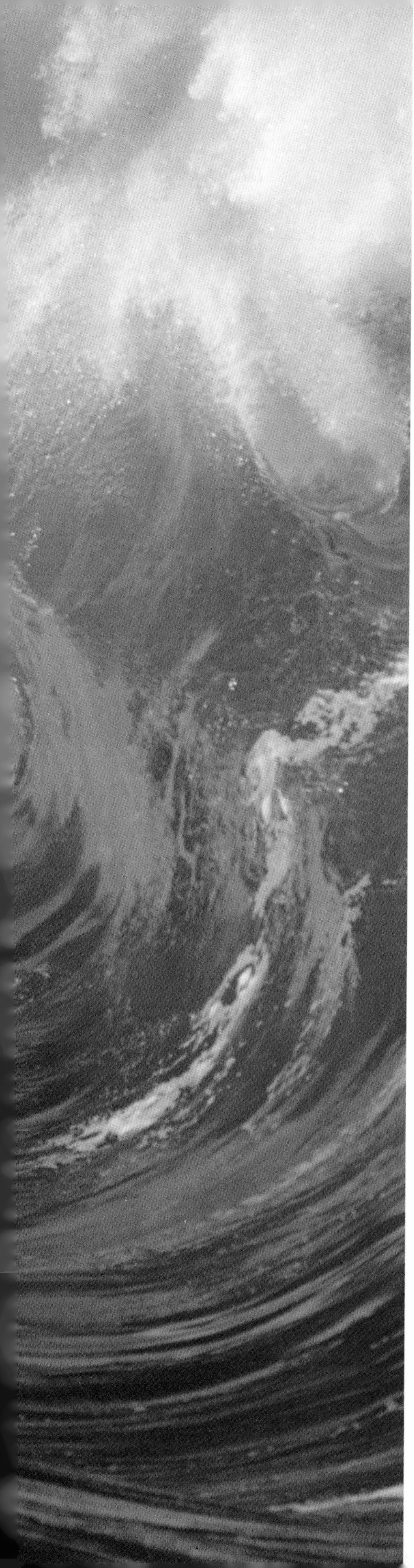

Ocean Planet

Earth is mostly covered in water. That is why it is known as the blue planet. There is a whole world to explore beneath the seas.

Seas and Oceans

Most of the water covering our planet is salt water. This includes Earth's seas and oceans.

Oceans

Oceans are the vast bodies of salt water that cover our planet between the continents. The Atlantic Ocean lies between Europe and the Americas. The other oceans are the Indian, the Pacific, the Arctic, and the Southern.

Earth's oceans cover more than 70 percent of its surface.

Seas

A sea is a body of water that is mostly surrounded by land. For example, the Mediterranean Sea is surrounded by southern Europe and northern Africa. It is connected to the Atlantic Ocean by a small opening called the Strait of Gibraltar.

The Mediterranean Sea is surrounded by land.

Clouds

The sun causes ocean water to evaporate. Air currents move that vapor into the atmosphere, where it condenses into clouds. Water droplets collide with one another in the clouds and combine to form larger drops. Then they fall to the ground as rain or snow.

Clouds that will bring rain or snow mainly form over oceans. The wind pushes them toward land.

Floating and Moving

To move forward in water, you have to cut through it by being hydrodynamic.

Floating on the Surface

How does a seabird rest on water without sinking? It can float because it is very light relative to its size. If the bird were dense, or heavy for its size, it would sink like a rock.

This gull is floating on the surface of the water.

Floating Just Below

People are denser than birds, but not dense enough to sink in salt water. A diver can float effortlessly just below the surface. To sink to the bottom, the diver would have to wear a weighted belt!

If you lie very still in the sea, you will float just below the surface, but you won't sink!

How to Dive

The human body is not designed to cut through water. When we dive, we use flippers to help us move forward. To avoid being slowed down by our arms, we hold them flat against the body or straight above the head.

This diver stretches out her arms and straightens her body to glide through the water.

Just the Right Spot

Fish are able to float in the sea at the exact depth they want. That's thanks to a pocket of gas in their bodies that acts like a small buoy. Water easily glides past either side of their streamlined bodies.

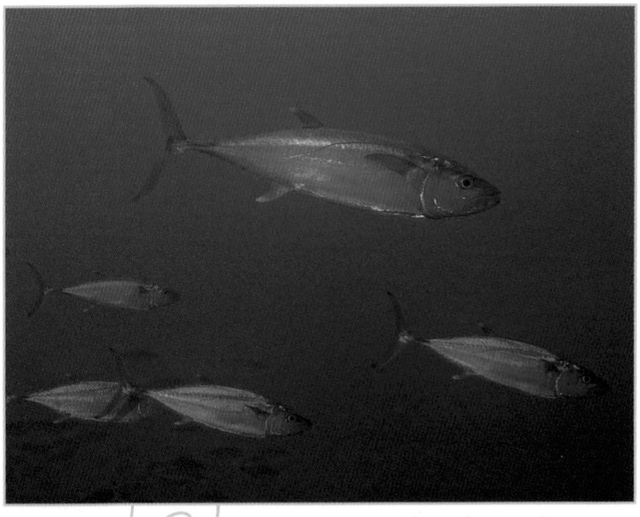

Tuna are fast swimmers. Their tails act like motors and push them forward.

Dolphins can swim as fast as 30 mph (48 km/h)!

Gliding Along

Any aquatic animals that can swim fast have streamlined shapes that cut through water. For example, dolphins have pointy noses and smooth bodies.

Low Tide, High Tide

Tides are the constant changes in the level of oceans. These changes may be a little or a lot. They are caused by the gravitational pull of the moon and the sun on Earth.

Low Tide

When the sea level goes down, it's called low tide. This is a good time to discover the small animals that live under rocks and in puddles.

At low tide, people can catch crabs and other shellfish.

Out of the Water

It's hard for aquatic animals to survive at low tide! Those that can move hide in holes or stay cool under algae. Those that are attached to rocks or other hard surfaces close their shells tightly to retain their water.

This green crab was surprised by the low tide. It will quickly try to hide under some seaweed.

At high tide, the leaves of the algae float and stand up straight. Aren't they pretty?

Open Up

During high tide, shellfish that are attached to hard surfaces open their shells halfway to take in fresh water. Mussels and barnacles can once again breathe and eat.

High Tide

When the water covers the rocks once again, algae begin to float and stand up straight. With their roots firmly attached to rocks, they sway in the waves. Together they create a sort of underwater forest.

Blennies come out of their holes and climb up on rocks to survey their surroundings. What strange fish!

Come Back Out

The animals that had hidden come back out. Crabs and lobsters look around for something to eat.

After having kept their shells closed for many hours, mussels can finally open up and breathe.

The Ocean's Wrath

The ocean is not always calm. When it is windy, waves appear. And a storm can really rile up the seas!

This windsurfer is being pushed forward by the wind.

Waves

Wind creates waves as it blows on the water. At first, they are just ripples on the water's surface. If the wind increases, you can see white foam called whitecaps on top of the waves.

Sea Swells

Sometimes the wind creates waves that spread very far. These are called sea swells. As they reach a beach, sea swells unfurl. The waves stand up straight, curl up, and break on the shore.

Swells crash on the beach.

Enormous waves crash against the coast repeatedly. Over time, these waves can cause rocks to break.

Storms

The windier it is, the stronger the waves become. Then a storm comes. Anyone in a boat should be careful! These large waves crash violently against the shore.

Cyclones

Strong tropical storms are called cyclones, hurricanes, or typhoons. The winds can be so violent that they blow away trees, cars, and roofs. The waves can be so large that they flood levees at ports and sink ships.

A storm has arrived. The danger is real. This truck could easily get swept away by the water.

Temperate Seas

Temperate oceans change with the rhythm of the seasons.

The Mediterranean

The Mediterranean Sea is not very cold, but it is especially prone to storms in the winter. The sea is often very clear so you can see right to the bottom from above the surface.

Look how clear the water is! You can see the sand and the dark spots on the rocks.

Large aquatic plants called posidonia need sunlight to live and grow.

Light Under the Sea

The sun's light easily penetrates clear water. That is why you can find meadows of aquatic plants growing very deep in these spots.

In Brittany, France, winter is often cloudy and stormy. But on a sunny summer day, the landscape is bursting with color!

The English Channel and the Atlantic

Clouds and rain from the ocean arrive on the Atlantic coast or at the English Channel. However, it is usually sunny in summer.

Marine Life

Unlike in the Mediterranean, most seawater is not completely clear. It is filled with tiny particles. Seaweed gets nutrients from the water. In turn, the seaweed serves as food for marine animals, such as crustaceans, shellfish, and fish.

Large seaweed grows well in shallow water where sunlight can penetrate the water.

Glacial Seas

Near the North and South Poles, the oceans get so cold that they turn to ice. This makes traveling and living there very difficult.

Ice Floes

When it gets very cold, the surface of the seawater freezes, forming sea ice. Large sheets of ice about 65 feet (20 meters) across or bigger are called ice floes. They can be up to 7 feet (2 meters) thick.

A special boat called an icebreaker is used to travel through sea ice.

Icebergs

There are huge glaciers in the polar regions. There, the ice slowly slides into the sea and giant blocks of ice break away. This creates icebergs—gigantic ice cubes floating in the sea!

Only a small portion of an iceberg is visible above the water. Most of it is hidden under the surface.

Seals

Seals in polar regions hunt in icy water. They climb back up on the ice floes to rest. That is also where they give birth to their babies.

A thick layer of fat keeps this Weddell seal from getting cold.

Although they are land-dwelling mammals, polar bears are excellent swimmers.

Polar Bears

Polar bears live on the ice floes and frozen ground in the North Pole, but they can also swim great distances. They don't get too cold thanks to their specialized fur and a layer of fat. A polar bear's diet consists primarily of seals.

Penguins

Some penguins live around the South Pole. They swim very fast and dive to catch fish. They may spend most of their lives in the icy waters. They climb up on icebergs or ice floes to rest.

These Adélie penguins are heading for the water—that's where they find all their food.

Tropical Seas

In tropical areas, the ocean is warm throughout the year. Magnificent coral reefs develop underwater.

These Polynesian fishermen are using an outrigger canoe with a float on one side.

Life in the Tropics

Although it is hot all year in the tropics, there is often a rainy season that brings storms. In some places, coconut palms grow along the beaches. Many people who live near the ocean make their living by fishing.

Coral Reefs

There is an extraordinary world to explore beneath the water's surface. All shapes of corals, fish of all colors…it may be the most beautiful show on Earth!

In the reef, all kinds of colorful fish swim among the corals.

Life in Paradise

It might be tempting to want to live on a tropical island. You might think it would be like being on a permanent vacation! But the people who live there still have to go to school and work—just like you and your family members!

People who live on tropical islands often have a boat for getting around, fishing, and even playing.

From the Surface to the Depths

Living creatures can be found in all the oceans and in any environment—from the coast to the deepest trenches.

The Coast

Plants and animals that live along the coastline may be under the water or above it. They have to be very hardy.

Changing Tides

Along the coasts, the sea rises and falls with the tides. Low tide can be a good time for you to explore!

Algae in tidal areas can withstand being exposed to the air for several hours a day.

Low Tides

In the Mediterranean, the tides are very low. The coastal area is merely a swath of land that is sometimes underwater and sometimes not.

When the Mediterranean is calm, the waves barely wet the rocks.

Salt Marshes

Salt marshes are large, flat areas that are sometimes underwater. Very special plants that are tolerant of salt grow there.

Plants must be very hardy to survive in salt marshes.

Sea Debris

The waves leave all kinds of things on the shore. These include algae, shells, shorebird feathers, small aquatic animals, and even garbage thrown into the sea by people.

Dead leaves and aquatic plants that were carried by the waves have piled up on this beach.

The Rocky Floor

The rocky ocean floor is full of hiding places. It also provides animals and plants that must be attached to something solid a great place to live.

The sun shines on the algae growing on these rocks.

A Carpet of Algae

Brown, green, and red algae grow on rocks that are exposed to light. When you look closely, it looks like a continuous carpet. Certain fish and sea urchins graze there.

Coral Reefs

Coral reefs are made up of animals that live attached to rocks. They come in many hues and are often very brightly colored.

These red sea fans look like bushes, but they are actually animals!

This brown-marbled grouper has made its home among the rocks in a small cave.

Living in the Rocks

Rocks are perfect for playing hide-and-seek! Animals use them as homes and as places to hide from enemies.

Immobile Animals

Plants, like algae, grow on rocks and hard surfaces. Many animals such as sponges, mussels, anemones, and corals also live attached to various surfaces.

Red coral is an animal. Each white "flower" is a mouth surrounded by tentacles.

Kelp Forests

Kelp forests sometimes grow on rocky ocean floors in temperate climates. Some algae can grow taller than a house!

Kelp's trunk-like stalk is called a stipe. It also has green or brown blades that look like leaves.

Underwater Forests

Large seaweed called kelp grows along the Pacific Coast. Standing on trunk-like stalks, these kelp grow close together to create what looks like a forest.

Under the Kelp Forest

Fish and crabs find hiding places and food in the shadow of the kelp. Other animals, like sponges, live permanently attached to the bottom of the seaweed.

Sea stars have found shelter in the shade of the kelp.

Sunlight filters through the blades of giant kelp.

Giant Kelp

Giant kelp is attached to the ocean floor. It has gas-filled bladders that help it stand upright in the water. These plants can grow as tall as 175 feet (53 meters) high!

Sand and Meadows

Sometimes beach sand extends under the sea, but it is not a desert. Entire meadows of sea grass grow there.

Moving Sand

Ocean waves cause rocks to crash into one another and other hard surfaces, breaking them into small pieces. This gravel gets rolled around by waves and becomes even smaller grains of sand. The waves and currents move the sand around.

Waves displace the sand on the ocean floor, creating ripples.

Living on the Sand

It is hard to see anything on the sandy ocean floor, but many animals live there. Some are flat and sand-colored. Others hide under the sand.

This flat fish is extremely well camouflaged!

Posidonia is a dark green aquatic plant that is found in the Mediterranean Sea. It can live on the sand.

Underwater Meadows

Algae cannot live in sand because they have to have a solid surface to hold on to. Unlike algae, aquatic plants can sink their roots into the sand. In some places, they form vast underwater meadows and beds of sea grass.

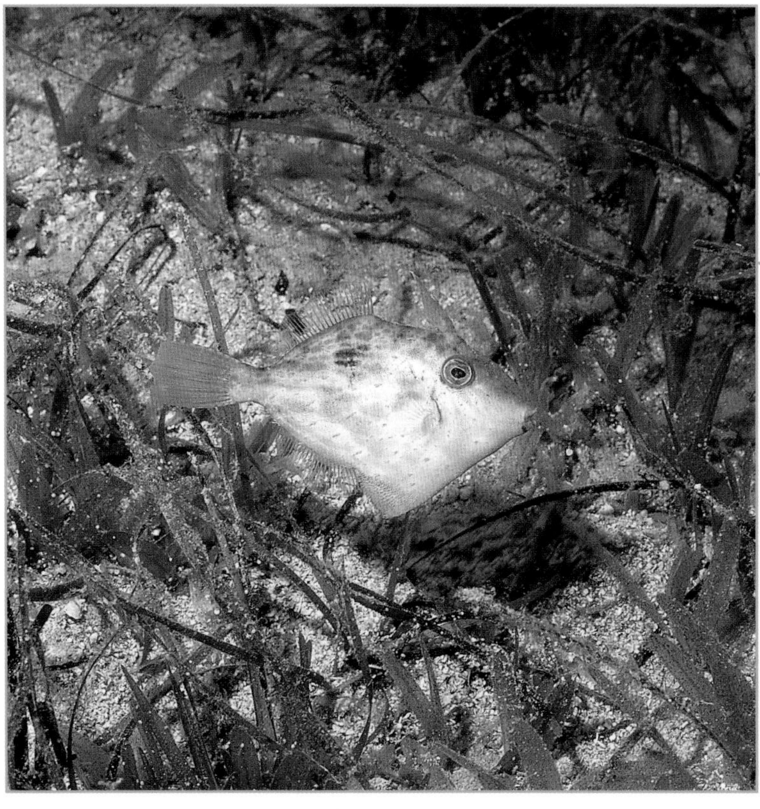

The bristletail filefish is easy to miss when it is hiding among green plants.

Living in the Sea Grass

Baby fish and other animals often hide in sea grass beds. If they are small enough, they can easily find hiding places there. Animals that live in the sea grass are sometimes very strange.

Coral Reefs

Coral reefs can be found in warm water. They are home to many animals of all shapes and colors.

Barrier Reefs

Some coral reefs form barriers in the water. Animals called corals construct them. The corals, which can't move, make limestone skeletons. That is how reefs have been growing for thousands of years.

Waves break on coral reefs just under the water's surface.

Sheltered by Corals

Corals come in all shapes and sizes. Multicolored fish and all sorts of animals live among them. Coral reefs are the richest underwater environment on our planet.

These fish are taking refuge in a clump of corals.

Coral Atolls

Corals live in warm, clear water. Since they need light, they form near the water's surface. Ring-shaped coral reefs that form around tropical islands are called atolls.

The waves break when they reach the coral reef around this island.

The Open Sea

Far from the coast, in the open sea, there is no shelter—only blue.... For the animals that live here, danger can come from anywhere!

Mirror Camouflage

Fish cannot be invisible. So they come up with other solutions. Some fish have silver skin that shines like a mirror. They reflect the blue color that surrounds them and take on the color of the sea.

See how these silvery barracuda appear to be blue like the sea?

Transparency

The best way to escape from your enemies is to not be seen. But how can that be avoided when there is nowhere to hide? Some animals, like jellyfish, are transparent. You can see through their bodies!

Jellyfish are transparent, so you have to be very close to see them.

These pilot fish are swimming under a big shark. You can recognize them by their black stripes.

Strange Shelters

In the open sea, fish often hide near floating objects, like tree branches, seaweed, or even cans. Pilot fish travel with sharks because that's how they get food. But swimming with the ocean's top predator probably offers some protection, too!

Sticking Together

It's not safe to be alone in the open sea. From small sardines to large dolphins, many ocean animals stay in groups of hundreds or even thousands. This is called living in a school or a pod.

Dolphins sometimes gather in groups of thousands. They are called superpods.

The Trenches

It is cold and dark at the bottom of the ocean—miles from the surface. Bizarre animals live there. Some even glow in the dark!

Blind Shrimp

Food is scarce in the abyss. To survive there, creatures must supplement what they manage to find in the deep with whatever sinks from the surface. Eyes are almost useless in the dark, so many deep-sea animals are almost blind.

Some shrimp, like this one, dig their burrows in the mud.

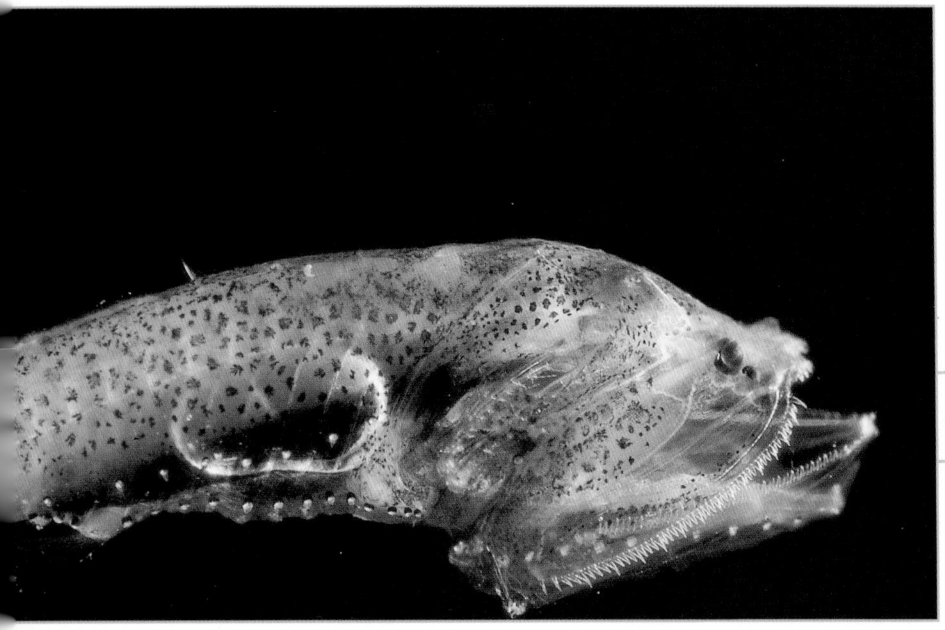

Lantern Fish

Deep in the ocean, fish swim in the darkness of trenches. Many have body parts that light up. They use these lights to communicate with one another and to capture prey.

Do you see the bright spots on this lantern fish's belly? Those are light-producing organs.

Dark Caves

Like in the abyss, it is often cold and dark deep inside underwater caves. That is why some fish that can survive at much greater depths live there.

This fish was found in absolute darkness more than 300 feet (91 meters) from the entrance of an underwater cave.

Smokers

There are two types of hot springs at the bottom of the ocean—white smokers and black smokers. The water coming out of these hydrothermal vents looks like smoke. That's where they get their name!

This is a black smoker. Can you see the crabs and fish nearby?

At Home on the Sea

Many people love the sea. Some like boating or fishing. Others enjoy a relaxing beach vacation.

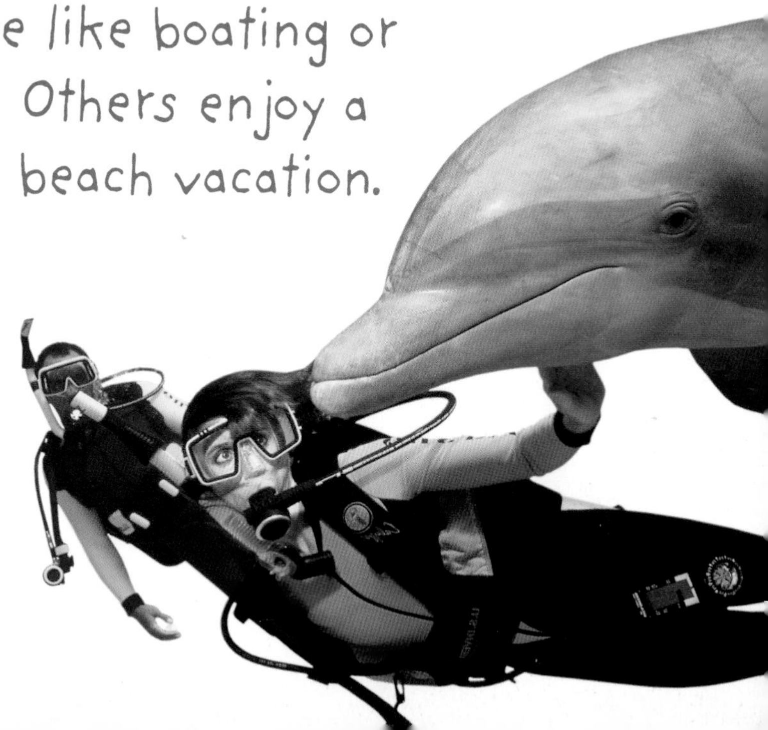

People of the Sea

From warm tropical coasts up to the icy North, there have always been people who make their living from the sea.

Mokens

The Moken people generally live near Myanmar and Thailand. They are sea nomads. For most of the year, they live on their wooden boats and travel along the coast. They catch fish and other seafood to eat and sell.

The Moken people travel in these sturdy wooden boats.

Inuits

Inuits live in cold arctic regions, including northern Canada, Alaska, and Greenland. For many long months, the sea is frozen over. They hunt seals and catch fish for food.

This man can still fish even when an ice floe covers the sea. All he needs is a hole in the ice.

Polynesians

The Polynesian islands are in the Pacific Ocean. The native people who live there are great fishermen. They invented a special trap—the fish can get in the pen, but they can't get out!

Fish traps can be made of wooden posts and wire fencing. They are very effective. Sometimes they even catch sharks!

Maldivians

The Maldives, in the Indian Ocean, are very low-lying islands. There are a variety of groups living there with many different cultures. Many people make a living by fishing.

Maldivian fishermen are at home on their small boats.

The Ocean's Bounty

All kinds of tasty fish can be caught in the ocean. And they are not the only "treasures" that may be found under the sea.

Local Fishing

Local fishermen are also known as small-scale fishermen. They usually fish near the coast aboard small sailing ships or boats. They lay down fish traps, nets, or lines on the ocean floor.

This fisherman caught a lot of fish in his small net.

Industrial Fishing

Industrial fishermen have large fishing boats. Some drag their nets on the ocean floor. Others use big nets to surround schools of fish. Some boats are like factories—they freeze the fish right on board!

On this trawler, an electric winch pulls up a net filled with fish.

These people are harvesting salt.

Sea Salt

Salt marshes are large, shallow basins that can be found along coasts. Saltwater comes into the marsh, then evaporates in the sun, leaving salt behind.

Pearl Oysters

Sometimes a small piece of dirt or sand gets stuck between the shells of a pearl oyster. It gets covered with layers of nacre and becomes a shiny ball called a pearl. This happens naturally. But some people insert dirt into oysters to help the process along!

People grow pearl oysters by hanging them from ropes underwater.

Ocean Travel

People have been navigating the world's oceans and seas for a very long time.

This is a catamaran. It is made up of two connected hulls.

Sailboats

For a long time, people navigated the sea with sailboats. Today these boats are primarily used for sports or leisure. It's nice to be moved forward by only the wind. All you can hear is the sound of the water gliding along the hull.

This motorboat goes fast, but it uses a lot of gas!

Motorboats

Motorboats are very practical because they allow you to travel even when there is no wind. However, they make more noise than sailboats. The motor turns a propeller that moves the boat forward.

Containers are stacked on the cargo deck of this ship. Each container is the size of a truck!

Cargo Ships

Cargo ships are big boats made to carry large loads. They go into ports to load and unload their goods. Some are designed to transport containers.

Cruise Ships

Some large vessels called oceanliners, or cruise ships, specialize in transporting passengers. When you go on a cruise for vacation, it is usually on an oceanliner.

Cruise ships make stops at various ports of call so passengers can visit them.

A Beach Vacation

It is so much fun to play in the sand and splash in the water! Of course, you must always be careful in the sun and the sea.

On the Sand

Beaches can be great places to play. You can dig big holes or make sand castles or sculptures. All you need is a shovel and a bucket.
To protect yourself from the sun, always wear sunscreen and a hat or even a T-shirt.

The risk of getting sunburned is stronger near the water. Don't forget your sunscreen!

At the Beach

It's fun to take a walk along the sand and look for seashells in all shapes and sizes. Every time you visit the beach, you can add to your collection!

Sometimes beaches can get very crowded. It can be hard to find a spot for your blanket!

This little girl is a pro at jumping over the waves!

In the Water

It is fun to wade in the water and splash in the waves, but be careful. If you are not a good swimmer, you should always stay close to an adult.

Water Sports

The beach is a great place to participate in many fun sports. Just watch out for swimmers!

Surfing

You need waves to go surfing. You also need great balance! Standing on a streamlined board as you steer it down the waves isn't easy.

This surfer is tethered to his surfboard. If he falls, he won't lose the board.

Inflatable Boats

Sometimes if the water isn't too crowded, you can float around in a small inflatable boat. Don't ever go floating alone, though. Someone should be there to make sure the wind and waves don't push your boat out to sea!

No need to worry about the waves with Daddy there!

Because windsurfers can go very fast, they should stay away from swimmers.

Windsurfing

A windsurfing board has a sail that catches the wind and helps the board glide over the water. You won't believe how fast they can go! Windsurfers can even jump over waves. But it takes skill to position the sail just right.

Personal Watercraft

A personal watercraft is like a small, fast motorboat. Some are meant to be ridden standing up, others sitting down. Both are fun—and noisy!

For the safety of swimmers, people often aren't allowed to ride personal watercraft near the beach.

People Underwater

All you need to explore underwater is a mask and a snorkel. If you want to stay underwater longer, you have to use scuba gear.

Underwater Cameras

Since the invention of scuba diving, we have learned a lot more about the underwater world. Photographers and filmmakers use waterproof cameras to get underwater footage.

An underwater video camera is housed inside a large waterproof box.

An instructor escorts two new divers through the water.

Diving

Scuba divers must train and get certified before they can dive on their own. They carry a tank of compressed air with a hose and a nozzle that delivers the air to their mouths. They can stay underwater for a long time.

A Mask and Snorkel

A mask can help you see clearly in the water. You can use a tube, called a snorkel, to breathe with your head underwater.

To be comfortable while snorkeling, you need a mask that fits your face properly and a snorkel that's not too long.

When snorkeling, you can spend hours looking at the ocean floor, especially if the water is warm!

Snorkeling

Snorkelers do not use air tanks. They can breathe through their snorkels when they are floating on the surface of the water. But they have to hold their breath to go down deeper.

A skilled free diver can stay underwater for several minutes.

Free Diving

Free diving is a dangerous sport. People dive deep underwater—without using a scuba tank—and stay there for several minutes at a time. They have to train very hard to hold their breath that long.

Exploring the Oceans

Scientists have been studying this fascinating realm for the past 200 years. The adventure continues today.

Submarines

Scientists can access the ocean depths in submarines. They study the rocks and strange animals that they encounter.

This submarine, called the *Nautile*, enables scientists to study the ocean floor.

Oceanography

The first oceanographers were adventurers! They invented devices for measuring depth, taking water samples, and capturing deep-sea animals.

This photo is from an oceanographic expedition in the 1800s.

This scientist is studying the condition of the corals.

Scientific Diving

Before scuba diving was invented, scientists could not observe aquatic animals underwater. Today it is easier to study corals and fish in their environment.

Fragile Oceans

The world's oceans are in danger because of pollution and overfishing. This cannot continue any longer. We need to start taking care of the oceans now!

Pollution

One type of visible pollution is littering. There are other kinds of pollution that aren't so easy to see—but they are very dangerous, too!

On Beaches

Waves wash garbage that is floating in the water onto the beach. Some garbage was thrown into the sea. Other litter washed into the sea from rivers. This is the most visible type of ocean pollution.

It takes many years for plastic to disappear!

In the Water

Plastic bags pose the most danger in the water. Sea turtles and dolphins think they are jellyfish and eat them. This can cause serious health problems and even death.

Floating bags are very harmful to marine animals.

Poisoned!

Beluga whales can be found in the Saint Lawrence River estuary in Canada. But this habitat has become unsafe. The river is polluted. When belugas ingest these toxic substances, they become sick.

Beluga whales in the Saint Lawrence River die from pollution in the water.

Chemical Waste

Sometimes chemical waste makes it into the water. It can't always be seen, but it is felt. Many of these chemicals pose great danger to the animals that live in the area.

Sometimes factories dump toxic materials into rivers. Eventually the toxins make it out to the ocean.

Oil Spills

Sometimes spilled oil can contaminate our coasts and make them very dirty. Even worse—the oil can kill marine wildlife.

Oil

A lot of oil can be found under the sea. Companies build platforms on the water and pump the oil up through pipes. If there is an accident or a leak, oil spreads out on the surface of the water. This is called an oil spill.

Platforms like this one are used to extract oil from under the sea.

Containment Booms

Oil containment booms act as a fence around an oil spill so the oil can be cleaned up. Of course, ideally, oil would never be spilled into the sea in the first place!

This floating boom keeps the oil slick from spreading out and affecting the coast.

This oil-covered penguin managed to make it back to the coast. For it to be saved, people will have to clean the penguin's feathers, warm it back up, and feed it.

Oil and Birds

An oil slick is floating on the sea. A seabird breaks through the surface of the water and gets stuck in the sticky black oil. It cannot get out. If no one comes to rescue the bird, it will die.

Oceans in Danger

The sea's resources are not limitless. Our waterways are being endangered by overfishing and overuse.

Overexploitation

Around the world, people often fish too much. They take more than they need or will even use. For example, some fishermen catch and kill sharks just for their fins. They throw away the rest of the sharks.

Hundreds of shark fins are on display for sale.

This whaler caught two blue whales in the Antarctic.

Whaling

Years ago, some whales were hunted almost to extinction. Today, in certain countries, many species are protected. Their numbers are slowly increasing. However, some countries continue to hunt them.

The Aral Sea still exists, but it's small and possibly toxic.

A Murdered Sea

The Aral Sea in Asia is an enormous lake that was fed by two large rivers. In the 1960s, the rivers were diverted so their water could irrigate crops. This has caused the sea level in the Aral to decrease by more than 65 feet (20 meters)!

Salt deposits have formed on the shore of Lake Assal.

Dying Seas

When one part of a sea becomes isolated, its water evaporates and becomes increasingly salty. The salt forms crusts on the seafloor and the shore. This is happening in the Dead Sea in Israel and Lake Assal in Djibouti.

Saving the Seas

So many things threaten our oceans. What can we do? Together we must find ways to save the seas.

Clean Ports

Today some ports are equipped to remove trash and liquid pollutants from water. New oil tankers must flush their tanks in a port and not at sea. Recreational boaters are no longer allowed to throw their waste into the ocean.

The water in this port is clear. All the garbage, septic waste, and dirty water have been removed.

Purifying the Water

The dirty water from our homes, gutters, and factories needs to be purified. Water purification plants remove any dangerous materials in the water before pumping it back into a river.

At water purification plants, dirty water is cleaned before being returned to nature.

These small-scale fishermen do not overexploit the sea. They know that they have to leave some fish today if they want to fish in the future.

Environmentally Friendly Fishing

To avoid overexploiting the seas' resources, we must go back to small-scale fishing methods. That means catching only what you need and using everything you catch.

There are all kinds of artificial reefs. They are designed to provide an optimal habitat for marine life.

Artificial Reefs

Some seabeds are naturally poor in resources. Artificial reefs can be set up in those places. Algae and, later, animals attach themselves to the reef. Within a few years, fish arrive.

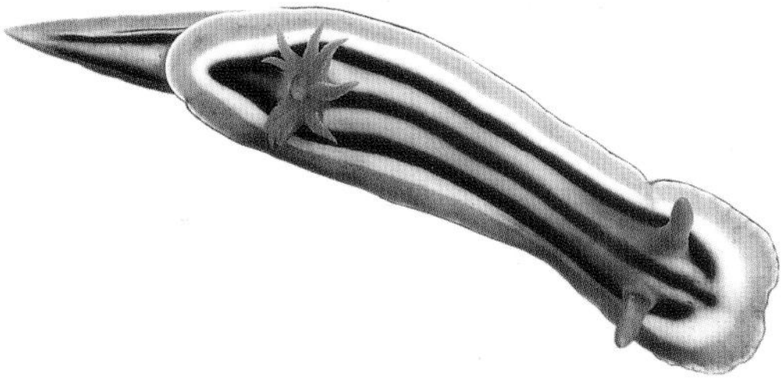

Who Lives Under the Sea?

Many animals live under the sea. Some swim or float. Others live on the bottom among the algae and sea grass.

They Swim

There are many ways of swimming. Some animals use their fins. Others use jet propulsion.

Using Fins

Fish swim with their fins. Their tails are called caudal or tail fins. Their pectoral fins are located on the sides of their body. They swim by moving their tail fins back and forth. They use their pectoral fins for steering and balance.

These wrasses are using their fins and flexible bodies to dart in all directions.

Jet Propulsion

The cuttlefish fills its pouch up with water. Then it squirts the water out through a tube in its stomach and darts away. This is like the engines on airplanes that push air behind them to move forward.

To move quickly, the cuttlefish pushes water through a tube called a siphon or funnel.

Sea turtles use their front flippers to swim. They use their hind flippers to steer.

Rowing Flippers

Sea turtles use their front flippers like oars. They swim very gracefully. It almost looks like they are flying through the water.

They Walk or Crawl

All kinds of animals live on the seafloor. They either walk or crawl along on the ground.

The hard shell covering a lobster's legs folds at the joints.

Articulated Legs

Lobsters have several legs, which—like the rest of their body—are protected by a hard shell. A lobster has articulated legs, so it can bend them when it walks.

Legs Under Their Arms?

Sea stars have small, flexible tubes under their arms that they use to move. It looks like they are gliding along the ocean floor, carried along by thousands of tiny feet.

When they are upside down, sea stars twist themselves and use their small, translucent feet to turn back over.

Crawling Along

Sea slugs slide along on the flattened part of their abdomen, called the foot. It looks like they are crawling.

This purple sea slug raises its "horned" head and eyes as it crawls along on its belly.

At the bottom of the sea, this gurnard slowly moves forward using its finger-like feet.

Walking Fish

Gurnards have appendages behind their heads that look like very thin fingers. They walk on their fins and use the appendages to move themselves along. They also use the appendages to hunt. They can feel vibrations made by worms or shrimp that are hiding.

Tufts of Hair

Some ringed worms are made up of several identical segments. Each segment has two tufts of stiff hairs called setae that they use to crawl along the ocean floor.

The bearded fireworm uses its white bristles for defense. They sting like glass needles.

Floating in the Sea

Animals and plants that float in the sea are collectively known as plankton. The animals are called zooplankton and the plants are phytoplankton.

What an Amazing Animal!

These bizarre translucent animals are called comb jellies. They float and drift in the sea, using their two thin, sticky tentacles to catch small prey.

The light-colored lines on the comb jelly's body are rows of small plates that help it swim.

Almost Invisible

Copepods are undoubtedly the most plentiful animals in oceans! Some types are no bigger than a comma. In plankton, there are animals and algae that are even smaller, which are impossible to see without a microscope!

Copepods are crustaceans that float in the open sea their whole lives.

Watch out!
Although the mauve stinger jellyfish looks pretty, it is actually quite dangerous. The filaments that trail behind it can inject toxins into your skin and hurt you!

Elegant Jellyfish

The umbrella-shaped top of a jellyfish's body is called the bell. A jellyfish can swim by contracting its bell, but it moves slowly and often drifts on currents. Some jellyfish have tentacles that sting like nettles!

Attached Animals

On the ocean floor, there are animals that never move. They are attached to rocks and other hard surfaces. They feed on what floats by in the water.

Strange Animals

Sponges form crusts of all colors with holes in them. To eat, they filter plantkton, bacteria, and other small foods from the water. Sea anemones stretch out their venomous tentacles to trap fish and plankton.

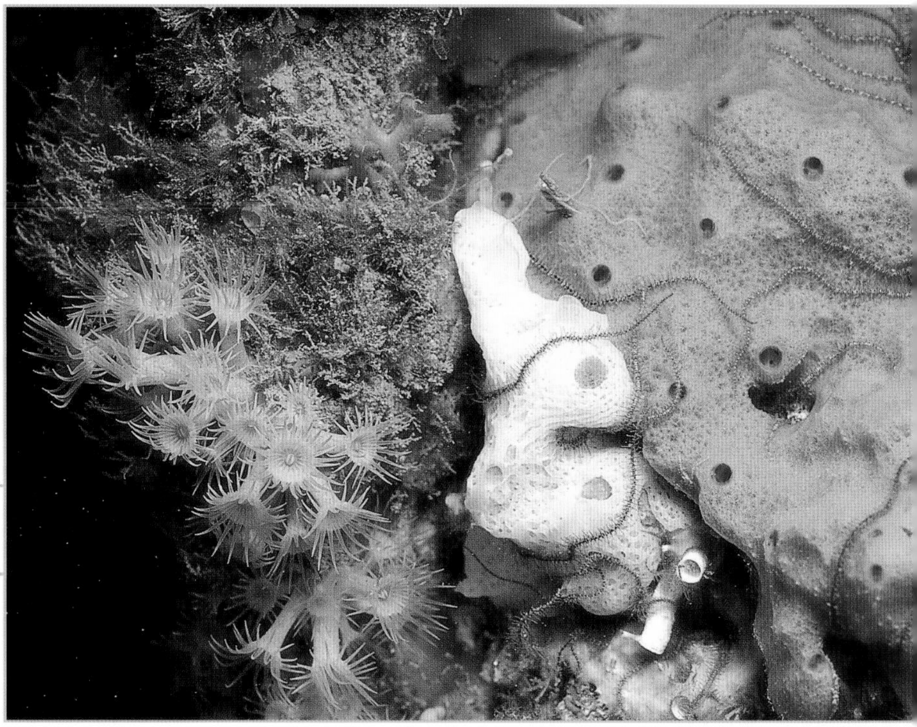

Do you see the sponges with all their little holes, and the yellow anemones with crown-like tentacles?

Many Mouths to Feed

Some sea anemones form colonies. Imagine lots of little anemones stuck together by their feet! That's what it is like.

Look at this soft coral. Each of its "flowers" is like a little sea anemone with its mouth surrounded by tentacles.

Two Holes for Filtering

Sea squirts have two holes. They use one to suck in seawater. After they filter microscopic food from the water, they squirt it out the second hole. Some sea squirts are transparent—you can see through their bodies!

These transparent sea squirts are filter feeders.

A Bouquet of Feathers

Some very unusual worms live in the sea. Their bodies are hidden in tubes out of which come odd, feathery bouquets. These plumes act like nets to capture tiny creatures floating in the water.

These are not feathers; they are a net. The spirograph worm stays hidden in its tube. It sticks out only the feathery plume on its head.

Marine Plants

Many plants grow on the ocean floor. There you can find algae in all shapes and colors, as well as sea grass meadows.

Green Algae

Green algae are usually found close to the shore, where there is plenty of light. Sometimes they detach and wash up on the beach.

These green algae look like salad greens. They're called sea lettuce.

This photo shows two types of brown algae. One has wide, twisting blades, and the other looks like a dense bush.

Brown Algae

Most algae live attached to a rock, a stone, or a shell, though some are free-floating. While some algae are very small, other varieties can reach heights of more than 100 feet (30 meters)!

Small bushes of red algae grow on a rock.

Red Algae

Red algae are not always red. Some are more maroon or purple. There are even types of red algae that are rock-hard because they contain limestone. They are usually pink.

Sea Grass

Most sea grass grows in sand. Like the grass that grows on land, sea grass has leaves and roots—it is not algae.

Cymodocea and posidonia are two kinds of aquatic plants.

Return to the Sea

Life began in the sea. Then reptiles, birds, and mammals colonized the earth. However, some of them returned to the sea.

Marine Reptiles

Most reptiles crawl when on solid ground. Marine reptiles can dive deep and spend hours underwater without coming up for air.

Saltwater Crocodiles

Saltwater crocodiles mostly live near coasts where rivers meet the sea. But they can also swim very far offshore. They grow to be quite large—20 feet (6 meters) long or more!

Saltwater crocodiles have large teeth. They use them to catch fish and land animals.

This sea snake's flattish body helps it glide through the water.

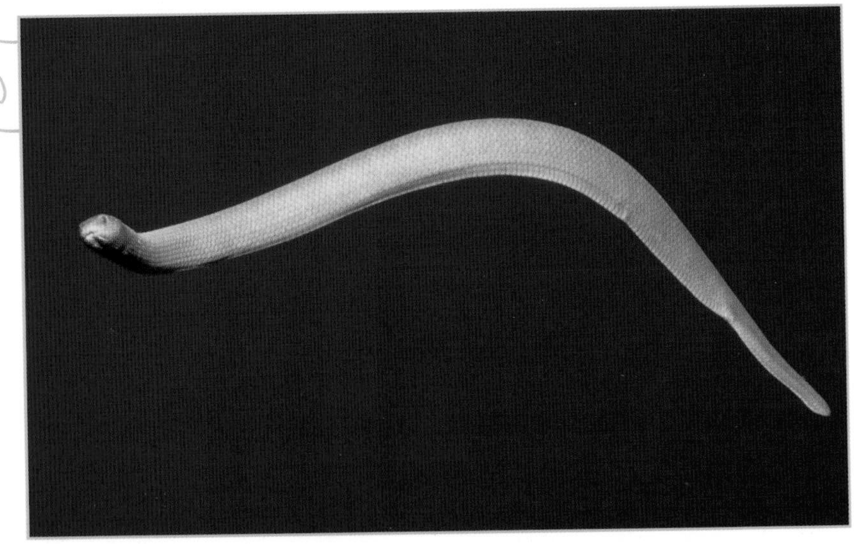

Sea Snakes

Sea snakes live in warm water. Some never go on land and even have their young in the water. Sea snakes are very venomous.

Sea Turtles

Sea turtles are easily distinguished by their paddle-like front flippers. Unlike some turtles, they cannot pull their heads into their shells. They can dive for extended periods, but must eventually resurface to breathe.

Sea turtles graze on grass on the seafloor. Some also like to eat jellyfish.

Two remoras are hitching a ride on this sea turtle. What strange fish!

Eggs in the Sand

Sea turtles must return to land to lay their eggs, which they bury in the sand. After hatching, baby sea turtles dig themselves out and run to the sea as fast as they can.

This green sea turtle has crawled up onto the beach at night. She is digging a hole in which she will lay her eggs.

Seabirds

Seabirds have wings for flying and gliding. They spend a lot of time on or near the water. Penguins are truly at home in the water. They can swim but don't fly.

Gliders

Many seabirds, like gulls and albatrosses, are gliders. They fly by soaring on the wind without flapping their wings. This allows them to travel great distances easily.

Albatrosses are skilled travelers. They can glide for hundreds of miles!

These puffins are very good at fishing. They resurface from diving with a beak full of fish!

Divers

Other seabirds flap their wings very fast when they fly. They use their short wings to swim when they dive to catch fish.

Clumsy on Land...

Penguins cannot fly, so they waddle along instead. Sometimes they must travel very far to get to the place where they lay their eggs and care for their babies.

It's slippery! This baby emperor penguin is not very steady on the ice. Luckily a parent is always there to help.

...Graceful Underwater

Although they look clumsy on land, penguins are expert swimmers. Using their wings as fins, they can swim as fast as the fish they hunt.

King penguins swim very fast. They shoot through the water like torpedoes!

Marine Mammals

Seals and sea lions live both on the land and in the water. Cetaceans, such as dolphins and whales, live only in the water.

Seals and Sea Lions

Seals and sea lions spend a great deal of time in the water. They enjoy resting on rocks. Sea lions have small external ears. Seals have holes in their heads for hearing.

Sea lions frolic in the water.

Dugongs

Dugongs are strange animals. From the front, they look a little like seals. But in the back, they have tails like those of dolphins or whales. They look like vacuum cleaners as they use their snouts to graze on sea grass.

Dugongs graze all day but must surface regularly to breathe.

Baleen Whales

Baleen whales don't have teeth. To eat, they swallow a large amount of water. Then they use their baleen plates to filter out the water while keeping shrimp or small fish behind. The blue whale is the largest animal on the planet.

This humpback whale is eating. Its throat expands as it fills with water.

Sperm whales have a very strange shape. Do you see the whale's long jaw under its head?

Sperm Whales

Sperm whales are the largest cetaceans with teeth. They can be 65 feet (20 meters) long—about as long as two buses! They also dive the deepest: more than 3,000 feet (914 meters)!

Dolphins

Dolphins have hydrodynamic bodies, made to cut through water easily. They swim very fast and hunt fish and squid. Dolphin calves are born underwater and quickly learn to hold their breath to dive.

Dolphins live in family groups called pods.

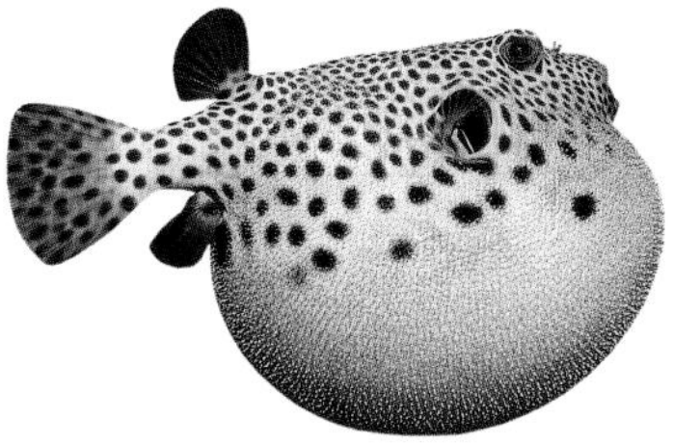

Attack and Defense

Marine animals have an arsenal of weapons at their disposal. They use them to track and capture their prey and to defend themselves from their enemies.

Specialized Teeth

Some marine animals have teeth that are adapted to what they eat. They may be pointed or rounded, thin or thick, and grow in a row or in a group.

Parrot's Beak

The parrot fish has very strange teeth. They are fused together to form a strong beak, which it uses to scrape algae from corals.

The parrot fish is named for its beak-like teeth.

The barracuda's impressive teeth help it catch fish.

Razor-Sharp Teeth

Barracudas eat other fish. They use their large, pointy teeth as hunting weapons to trap their prey.

A Toothy Smile

Since dolphins have neither hands nor nets, they must catch fish with their teeth. They don't use their pointy teeth for chewing, though. They swallow their prey whole.

This dolphin looks like it is smiling. Look at all those teeth!

Pincers and Suckers

Some marine animals possess very special weapons to attack or to defend themselves. These include suckers that they use to stick to things, and pincers that they use to pinch things.

Pincers

Lobsters are crustaceans. Some are armed with two enormous pincers. One is thin and can cut like scissors. The other is thick and strong enough to crush a shell.

This lobster's pincers serve different purposes. One is made for crushing, and the other, for cutting.

Small Pincers

Shrimp are also crustaceans, but their pincers are less formidable than a lobster's. Still, they are very useful. Shrimp use them for pecking for food among rocks and for grooming themselves.

Shrimp use their delicate pincers to catch all kinds of tiny foods.

An octopus uses its suctions cups for many things. It can use them to move over surfaces and to feel, hold, or rip things.

Suckers

Octopuses are truly extraordinary animals. They have no bones, only muscles. Their long arms, called tentacles, have hundreds of suckers.

Pincers Everywhere!

Horseshoe crabs are curious creatures that look like upside-down skillets. They have five pairs of legs and a set of pincers. They use their pincers to grab food and move it to their mouth.

This horseshoe crab has pincers on all of its legs. The crab's legs are usually hidden under its shell.

Chemical Defenses

How can an animal defend itself if it can't run away? It can use toxic or unpleasant substances.

Stinging Tentacles

The sea anemone has stinging tentacles. They burn like nettles. That is because their skin contains a type of venom that can kill the small marine animals they eat.

This shrimp is caught in the venomous tentacles of a sea anemone.

Venomous Spikes

Sea slugs can be a lot more colorful than their terrestrial cousins. Some of them taste so bad that other animals won't eat them. Some sea slugs have venom in the long outgrowths on their backs.

The orange protrusions on this sea slug are venomous.

Venomous Skin

Marine animals that live attached to solid surfaces often produce toxic or unpleasant substances. They taste so bad that almost nothing eats them. Some fish, like the puffer fish, are also poisonous. Its skin contains a lethal poison.

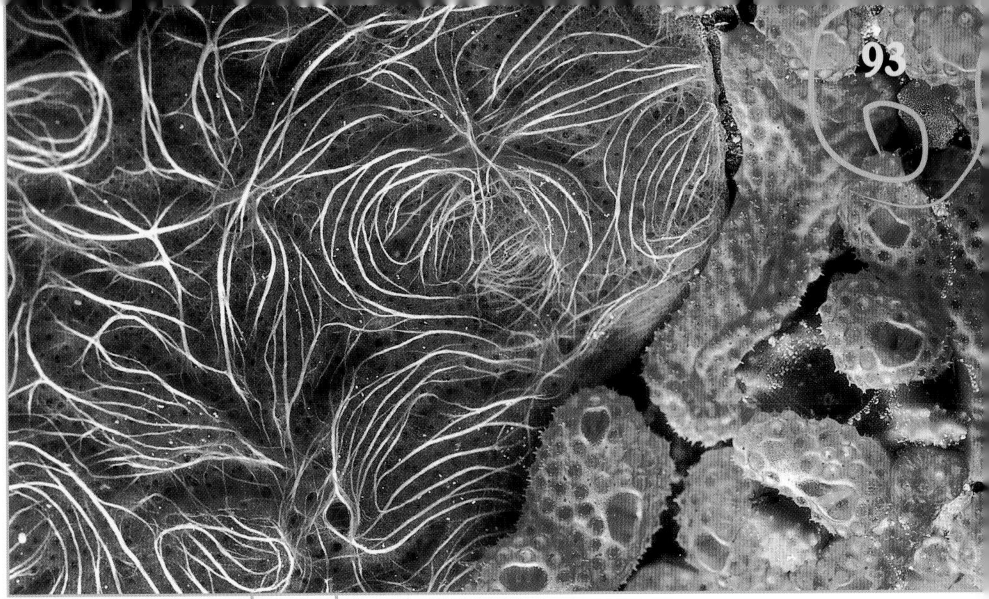

These sponges don't have to worry about getting eaten—they taste terrible!

This dwarf puffer fish may look cute, but if you eat one, it might kill you.

Repulsing Threads

When attacked, some sea cucumbers send out threadlike white filaments that stick to the predator and irritate its skin. After finally untangling itself from the filaments, the predator usually swims away.

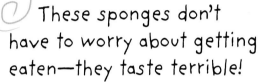

A sea cucumber's white filaments are a defense mechanism. They come out only when the animal is threatened.

Spiky Thorns

If you touch these animals, you will regret it! They are covered in spikes. That is their defense.

Crown-of-Thorns

The crown-of-thorns sea star has between eight and 21 arms. It is challenging to count them, though, since they are covered with large, thorny spikes. Ouch!

This creature is called crown-of-thorns. It's hard to tell it's a sea star.

Ball of Spikes

The porcupine fish has a surprising reaction to danger. It sucks in so much water that it blows up like a balloon! The porcupine fish is covered in spikes, so when it is "inflated," it is nearly impossible for it to be eaten.

This porcupine fish inflated itself because it was scared. Who would attack a spiny ball like this?

Tricky Spines

This triggerfish has spines on its back and belly. It uses those spines to wedge itself into small spaces. That makes it difficult for a predator to catch the fish.

This pretty triggerfish is well-protected. Do you see the imposing, thorny spine on its back?

Hidden in the Rocks

In the sea, hide-and-seek is not really a game. Knowing how to hide is a matter of life and death.

When camouflaged, this scorpion fish looks just like a rock. See if you can find its tail and eye.

Like a Rock

Sitting on a rock, this scorpion fish becomes almost invisible. It is the same color as the ocean floor and has little pieces of skin that look like algae. Predators could easily swim right past without noticing it at all.

Coat of Algae

A spider crab's shell is covered in spikes. The crab uses its pincers to tear off bits of algae and place them on its back. This coat of algae keeps the crab well hidden.

This spider crab looks like it has a garden on its back.

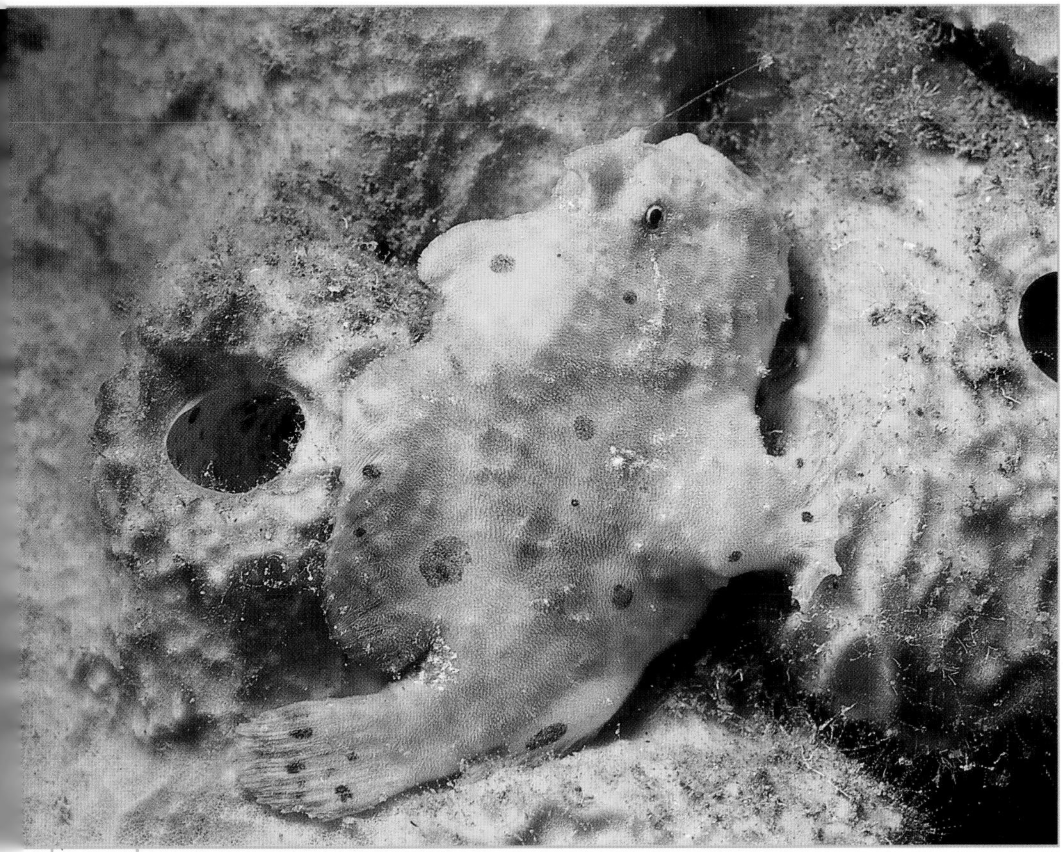

Do you see the frogfish hiding on the yellow sponge? It has funny fins that look like feet.

Colorful but Invisible

You really have to know what to look for to see this fish! Frogfish can be red, yellow, black, or white, but they blend so well into their surroundings that they can be hard to see. Frogfish are poor swimmers—they get around by walking on their fins.

Camouflage Champion

An octopus can instantly change its skin color to blend in with its environment. It can also make its body look like seaweed-covered rocks. Octopuses are underwater camouflage champions!

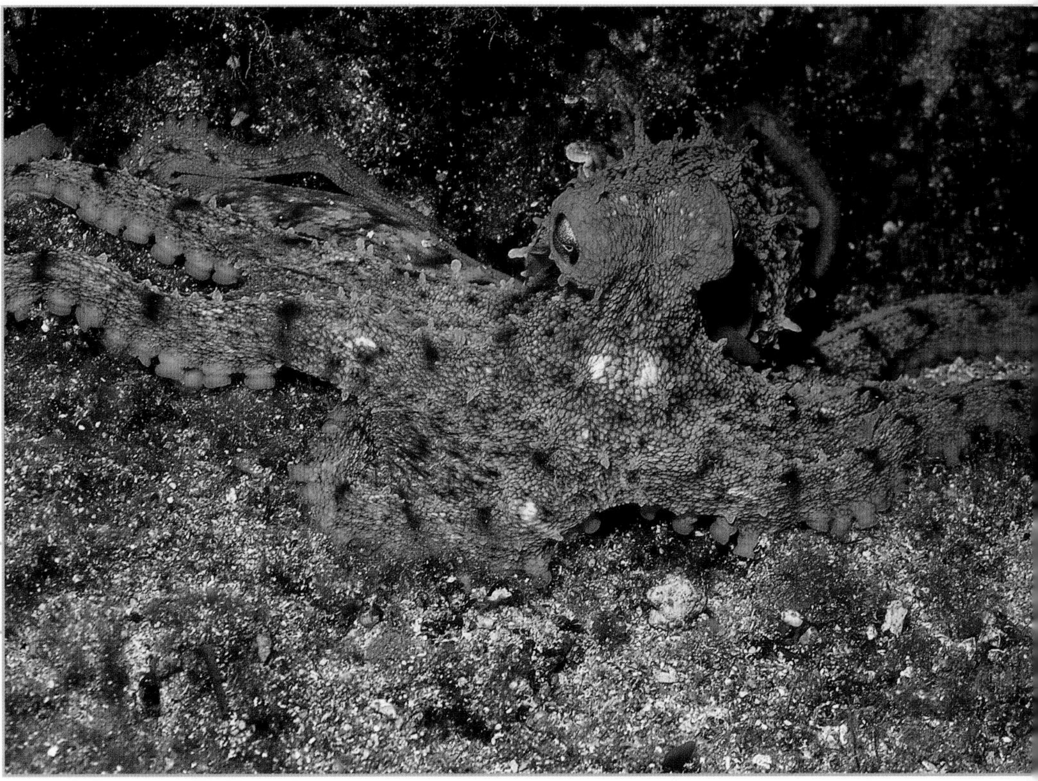

This octopus avoids detection by mimicking its surroundings.

Hidden in the Sand

Some animals prefer to hide on the sand instead of under it. If you want to hide on top of the sand, you have to be flat and sand-colored.

Superflat

Sandy ocean floors are flat, and so are the fish that live there. They can blend in well. Often, they cover themselves with a little sand, and then only their eyes can be seen!

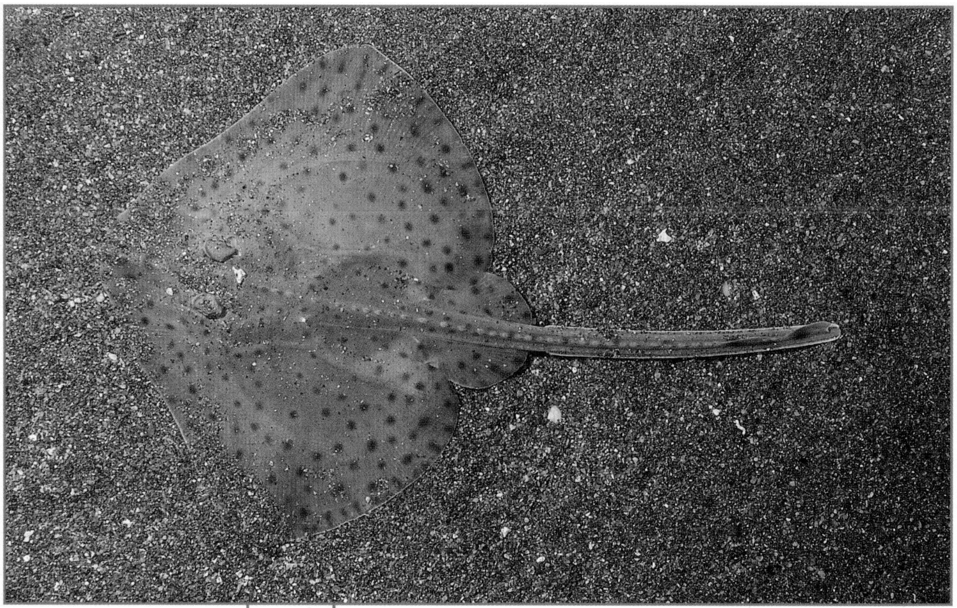

Stingrays are very flat fish. Only their eyes stick out.

Sand-Colored

Fish, crabs, and shrimp can all be sand-colored. Often they look like they have grains of sand drawn on their bodies. Some can even change their color to match the surrounding sand.

This crab is quite flat and matches the sand almost exactly.

A pearly razor fish sticks its head out of the sand where it was hiding.

Diving Fish

Fish usually swim in water. Razor fish also swim in the sand! When frightened, they dive, head first, into the sand to hide. They will only come out once they think the danger has passed.

Burrowing Sea Star

The red comb star has small tubes under its arms. It uses them to dig into the sand and burrow. Once under the sand, it disappears completely.

Soon this sea star will be completely covered by sand.

Deception

These fish don't hide from danger. Instead, they use optical illusions to confuse predators.

Fake Eyes

Butterfly fish have a black spot on the back of their bodies that looks like an eye. Predators think the fish will swim away in one direction, and it ends up going the opposite way!

Close your eyes halfway and try to see the butterfly fish's eye. Which jumps out at you—the real one or the fake one?

Black-and-white stripes provide camouflage for the damselfish.

"Broken" Shapes

When you look at the striped damselfish, the main thing you notice are its black-and-white stripes. But it is difficult to make out the fish's body. It's as if its shape were "broken" by the contrasting colors.

Lures

Lionfish have two fake fish on their heads that they use as lures, like fishermen do. When hunting, the lionfish hides its entire body except for the lures to attract other fish.

Each of the lionfish's lures is oval shaped and has a spot. Hungry fish approach for a meal and get eaten themselves instead!

In Disguise

One of the best ways to stay safe is to pretend to be something you're not—like a boring piece of seaweed or a dangerous animal.

Like a Blade of Grass

Shrimp or fish that look like blades of grass love to hide in the sea grass. They are a similar color and thickness. They hide along the length of the leaves to blend in even more.

Can you see this astonishing green shrimp? It looks like a blade of sea grass.

These dead leaves are really fish! Can you see their eyes and mouths?

Dead Leaves?

Some fish have an uncanny resemblance to dead leaves. They are impossible to spot—even against a clear background. When they swim, they look like drifting leaves.

A dwarf puffer fish's skin and several organs contain toxins. That is why no predators try to eat them!

Imitation

Some harmless fish imitate dangerous or toxic fish so predators won't bother them. For example, the mimic filefish is modeled after an inedible puffer fish.

The mimic filefish is safe to eat. But predators confuse it with a poisonous puffer, so they leave the filefish alone!

Social Life

It can be hard to survive alone. Many animals live in groups or join forces with other species. Some of these relationships are very beneficial.

Living in a Group

Some animals live alone. Others need the security of a group. It is easier to escape from your enemies if there are a lot of you.

When fish travel in schools, there are hundreds of eyes to scan the water for danger.

Living Together

Butterfly fish often live in couples: a male and a female. If there is danger, they will often separate to hide and then meet up again later. With their bright colors, they are easy to see!

Wherever you go, I will follow! Mr. and Mrs. Butterfly Fish always swim together.

Schools of Fish

Many fish live in groups called schools that can include thousands of fish. Some fish live in schools all the time. Others do so only occasionally.

Society Life

Dolphins always live in groups. Each group of dolphins has its own customs, which the adults transmit to the youngest dolphins. Like you, dolphins must learn the rules of life in a society.

These spinner dolphins know each member of their group. They use sound to communicate with one another.

A House That Stings

Sea anemones can sting. Yet some animals take shelter among their venomous tentacles.

Stinging Home

Sea anemones use their stinging tentacles to kill small fish to eat. However, some animals know how to hang out with the anemones without getting stung.

In warm waters, anemones and clown fish live together.

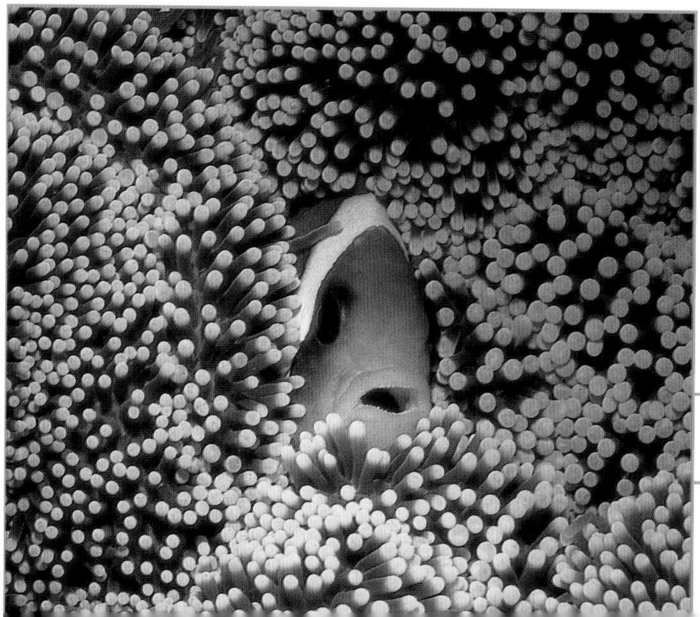

How to Not Get Stung

Clown fish begin by rubbing up against the anemone multiple times. Little by little, the clown fish becomes covered in the anemone's mucus. Once the clown fish is covered with the anemone's scent, it is no longer at risk for getting stung.

Clown fish routinely swim among deadly tentacles.

In the Mediterranean

The speckled goby also lives near sea anemones. When this fish hides beneath the anemone's stinging tentacles, it is impossible to catch it without getting stung.

When frightened, the speckled goby slips under the nearest anemone tentacles.

Porcelain anemone crabs catch small prey using their arms, which look like nets.

Anemone Crabs

Small porcelain anemone crabs live in warm waters. They station themselves on carpet anemones, which have tons of very short tentacles.

Anemone Shrimp

When anemone shrimp molt and lose their old shells, it takes them several hours to cover themselves in anemone mucus again. If they are not careful, they will get stung!

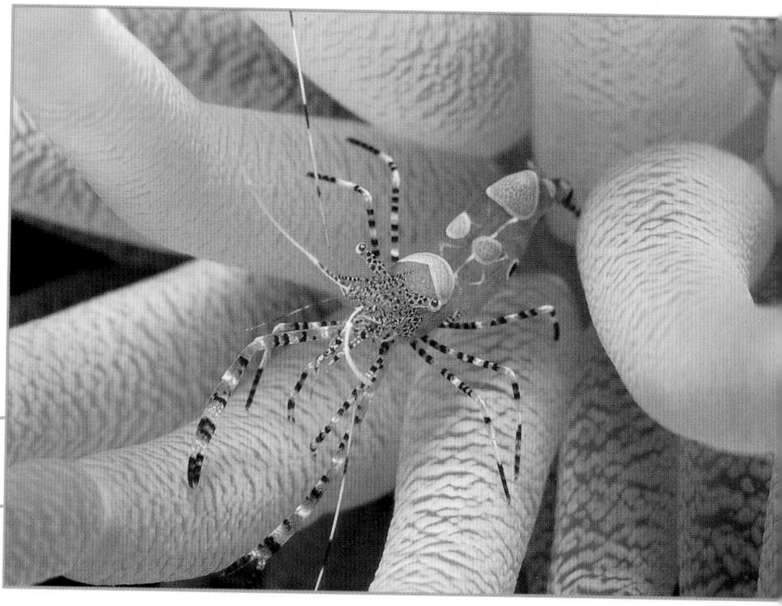

This pretty translucent shrimp is covering itself in anemone mucus so it will not be stung.

Roommates

Once you find a good shelter, you can keep it for yourself or share it. Some marine animals cannot live without a roommate.

Sharing Burrows

A fish is sitting on the sand in front of a hole near a coral reef. It's a goby, and if you look closely, you will see that it is not alone. A shrimp is sharing the burrow.

This shrimp and this goby are sharing the same burrow in the sand. In case there is danger, they both disappear into the safety of the hole.

While it works, the shrimp keeps one antenna in contact with the goby.

Sharing Chores

All day, the shrimp digs out the burrow, removes sand, and shores up the entrance with gravel while the goby appears to be doing nothing. The goby is actually monitoring their environment. At the slightest sign of danger, the goby warns the shrimp by nudging it.

This slipper lobster and moray eel are sharing the same hole—one on the floor and one on the ceiling.

Happy Together

Sometimes very different animals find that they both like the same hole. If they don't bother each other, they can share the space. That is why you sometimes see a conger eel with a moray eel or a lobster.

Guest Rooms

Shrimp, fish, and other marine animals like to hide in holes in rocks because they make good shelters. If their house is big enough, they are happy to share it with other animals.

These shrimp have found a safe place to share. They will come out at night to hunt for food.

At Your Service

Sometimes you can see fish that look like they are waiting in line. They are waiting their turn at the "service station" of a cleaner shrimp or fish.

A cleaner shrimp is looking for leftover food particles in this eel's mouth.

Say Ahhh...

This eel is visiting a cleaner shrimp. The eel opens its mouth. The tiny shrimp climbs onto the eel to make sure there are no small parasites around its eyes. Then the shrimp decides to clean the eel's teeth.

Want a Manicure?

Cleaner shrimp are always willing to be of service—even to humans. If you gently show a cleaner shrimp your hand, it will carefully inspect it and clean it off nicely.

What a dirty finger! This looks like a job for a cleaner shrimp!

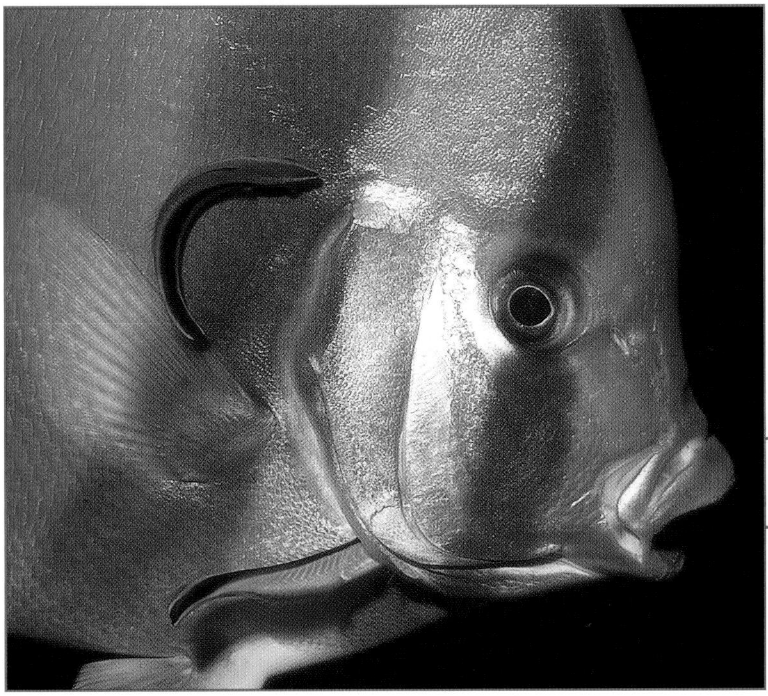

Cleaner Fish

Small cleaner fish can be recognized by their distinctive blue and black coloring. They feed on small parasites that are stuck on the skin or gills of other fish. They also clean other fish's wounds.

This large fish is opening its operculum so that the cleaner wrasse can inspect the gills underneath.

Time for a Cleaning

Cleaner wrasse love to clean inside mouths. In addition to yummy parasites, they find leftover food stuck between teeth. They are not at risk because no fish wants to eat its dentist!

A cleaner wrasse is cleaning another fish's mouth. It can't be afraid of getting bitten!

Underwater Babies

Baby dolphins and seals are easy to recognize, but what do the babies of other marine animals look like?

Drifting Larvae

Among aquatic animals, the babies are very different from the adults. They are tiny and transparent, and float in the water. It's a dangerous adventure!

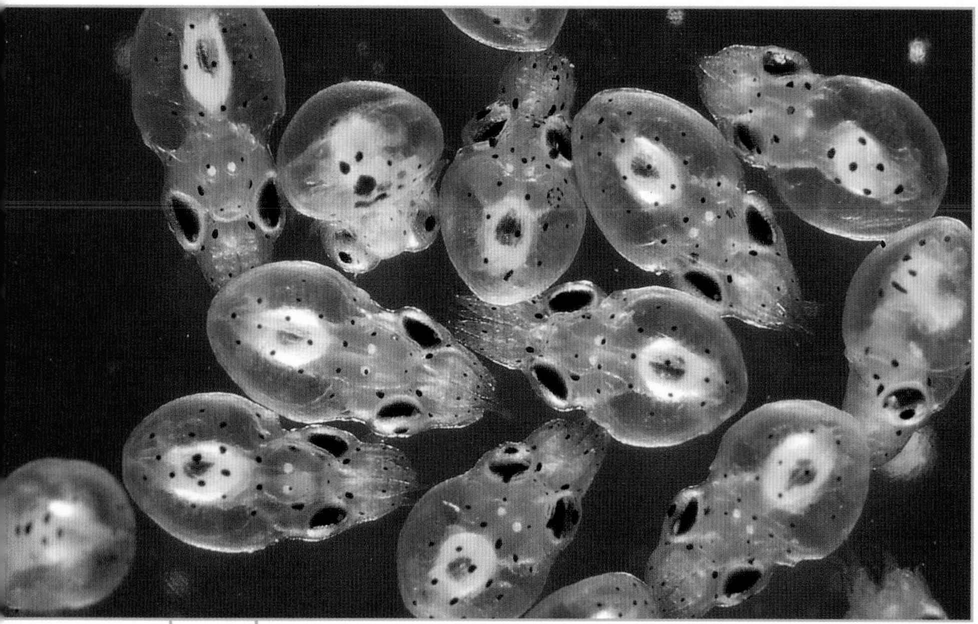

Some baby octopuses are transparent. These have small dark spots.

Baby Octopuses

Newly hatched baby octopuses are very small. They have large eyes and short tentacles. They swim backward by pushing water out of their pouches. They swim around like this before heading to the seafloor.

Sea Urchin Larvae

This funny-looking thing is a baby sea urchin! Since they are so different from the adults, they are called larvae. Many marine animals have astonishing larvae that float in the water before metamorphosis.

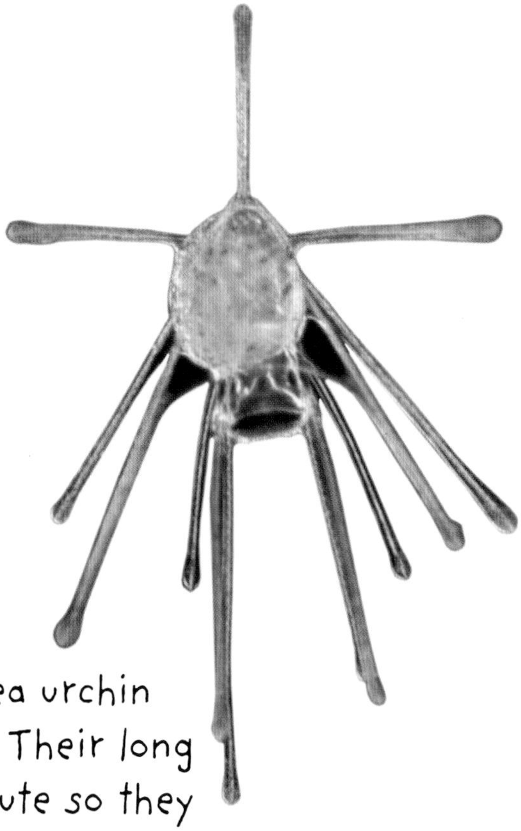

You can hardly see sea urchin larvae with the naked eye. Their long rods form a sort of parachute so they won't sink to the bottom of the sea.

Spawning in Open Water

When some fish mate, the male and female move away from the bottom of the sea and come together. This is called spawning. The female releases her eggs; the male, his sperm.

These are tropical wrasse. The female is smaller and does not have the male's bright colors.

Floating Eggs

The sperm fertilizes the eggs that will become baby fish. In some species, these tiny, transparent eggs float in the sea.

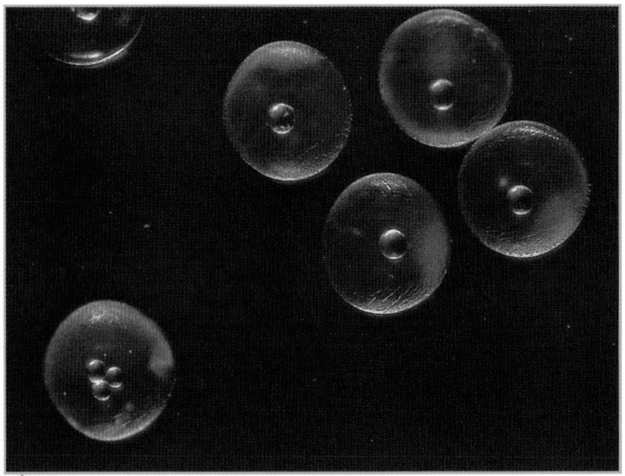

These fish eggs contain a drop of oil that makes them float.

Transparent Fry

After a few days, the eggs hatch. The baby fish mature and grow larger. Then these "fry" become capable of swimming and feeding themselves.

This fry spent weeks in the open water before coming to the bottom.

Distant Reproduction

For many marine animals, the males never meet the females, so they cannot mate. How do they make babies?

Fertilization in the Water

In the case of urchins and many other bottom-dwelling animals, the eggs and sperm are simply released into the water in hopes that they will find each other.

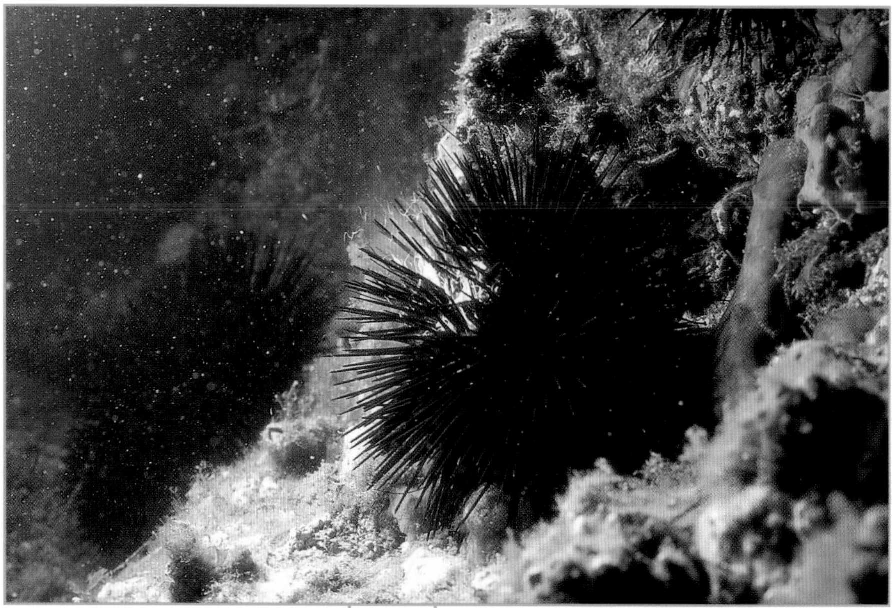

The sperm of this male urchin form a white cloud. They are ready to fertilize eggs.

The floating red dots are a female sea urchin's eggs.

Making Babies

In all animal species, it is the female that produces the eggs, and the male, the sperm. To become a baby, an egg must first be fertilized by a sperm. It's not always easy to make them meet up.

This is a male sea star perched as high as possible. The small white specks he is releasing contain thousands of sperm.

Stand Up Tall

Sea cucumbers and sea stars stretch themselves up high so their eggs or sperm will disperse well in the current.

Coral Spawning

In order to reproduce, some corals that are attached to rocks release their eggs and sperm into the ocean current. In certain tropical reefs, all the corals reproduce at the same time, so the sea is full of coral eggs.

This Mediterranean soft coral releases thousands of small pink larvae.

Caring Fathers

In certain types of fish, the males clean, protect, and care for the eggs. You could say they brood like mother hens!

A clown fish guards its eggs.

Big Deposit

Some fish, such as clown fish, deposit their eggs on a hard surface. They don't abandon them, though—the male cares for them and watches over them.

Larvae in the Open Sea

At birth, clown fish are transparent. They drift in the water. Once they have grown a bit, they look for sea anemones to live in. That is when they take on their orange-and-white appearance.

Before finding its anemone, this clown fish larva spent one or two weeks in the open water.

Eggs on Your Stomach

The female pipefish attaches her eggs to the male's birth pouch, which is on his belly. Then it is up to him to carry and protect them until they hatch.

It looks like a string, but this pipefish is a real fish. It's carrying its eggs in a birth pouch.

Eggs in a Pouch

Male sea horses carry the babies! Males have large pouches on their bellies into which females lay their eggs. After several weeks, the male "gives birth"—sometimes to hundreds of babies.

What a belly! The baby sea horses are going to come out of their dad's pouch soon.

Eggs in the Mouth

The way cardinal fish protect their eggs is quite surprising. The male keeps the fertilized eggs in his mouth! He has to keep them there until they hatch. During the entire time, he cannot eat anything.

This cardinal fish dad has his mouth full of the eggs he is protecting.

Watchful Moms

In the ocean, very few mothers care for their babies. There are exceptions, though, especially among marine mammals.

Mama Octopus

A mother octopus lays her eggs in a hole in the rock. There are thousands of eggs and each one is about as large as a grain of rice. She will watch over them and protect them from predators until they hatch.

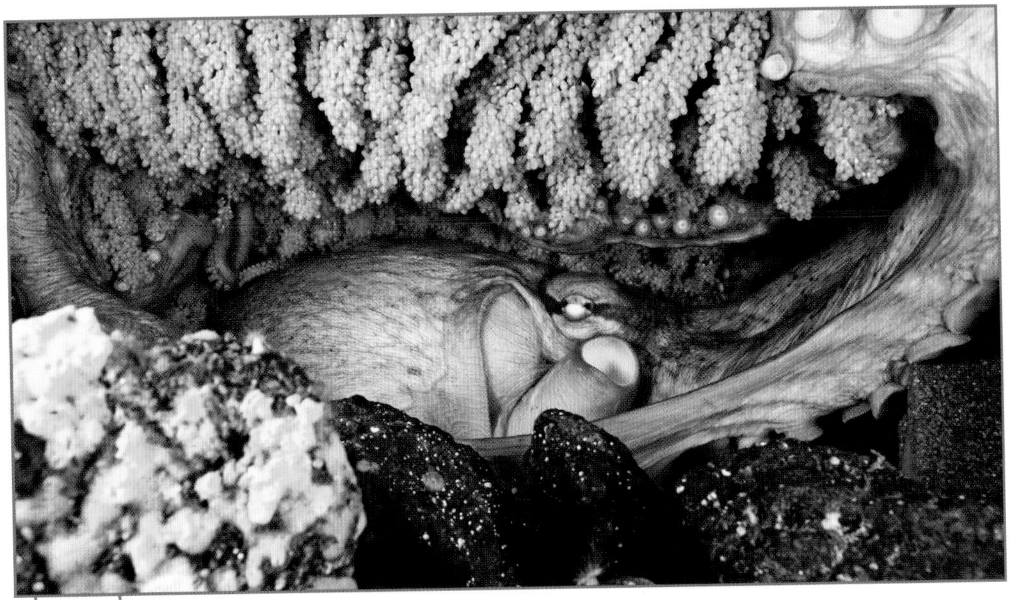

The mother octopus uses her tentacles to carefully clean her eggs.

Mama Dolphin

When a mother dolphin gives birth, she brings her baby to the surface of the water so it can breathe. After about six hours, she gives it milk to drink.

The baby dolphin rubs up against its mom, and she cuddles it with her fins.

Mama Otter

Baby sea otters are able to float from birth, but this one prefers to ride on its mom's warm tummy. Otters often swim on their backs. In the case of a mom, this makes it easier for her baby to nurse, sleep, or play.

This baby sea otter is being lazy! At two months, it is old enough to swim on its own.

Index

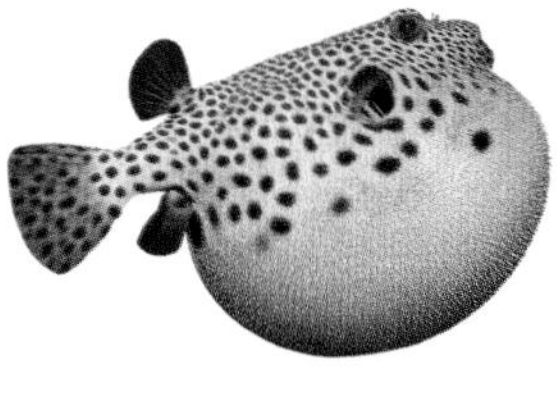

Photo Credits

All photos by PATRICK LOUISY except:

CORBIS

A. Rousse: p. 5, 115 (t); S. Wilkings: p. 8; BloomImage: p. 9; T. Van Sant: p. 10 (b); O. Van Der Wal: p. 11; L. Kennedy: p. 17 (t); J. Reed: p. 17 (b); R. White: p. 20 (t), 39 (b), 54 (t); P. A. Souders: p. 20 (b), 83 (t), 85 (t); R. Price: p. 21 (t); W. P. Conway: p. 21 (c); Th. Allofs/ZEFA: p. 21 (b); T. Bernhard: p. 24; R. A. Clevenger: p. 31; N. Rabinowitz: p. 35; A. Griffiths: p. 37 (b); P. Perrin/Corbis Sygma: p. 40; Y. Forestier/Sygma: p. 41 (t); S. Frink: p. 41 (b), 80 (b), 84 (t); P. Perrin: p. 42 (t); J. Jackson/Robert Harding World Imagery: p. 42 (b); J. W. Rogers: p. 44 (b); F. Soltan/Sygma: p. 45 (t); P. Blakely/SABA: p. 47 (t); O. Franken: p. 48 (b); A. Scott/ZEFA: p. 50 (b); K. Weatherly: p. 50 (t); P. Ward: p. 51 (b); M. Harvey: p. 56; W. Lawler/EcoScene: p. 59 (b); J.-L. Atlan/Sygma: p. 60 (b); M. Harvey/Gallo Images: p. 61; J. L. Rotman: p. 62 (t), 114, 122 (b); P. Johnson: p. 62 (b); K. Nomachi: p. 63 (t); K. Huntt: p. 64 (t); J. Sugar: p. 64 (b); P. Guttman: p. 78; T. Bernhard/ZEFA: p. 80 (t); K. Schafer: p. 82 (t); M. Buxton/Papilio: p. 82 (b); T. Davis: p 83 (b); D. Scott: p. 85 (c), 109 (c); S. Westmorland: p. 86, 105 (b), 122 (t); G. Bell/ZEFA: p. 104, 113 (b); R. Yin: p. 108 (c), 109 (c); B. D. Cole: p.115 (b); D. P. Wilson/Franck Lane Picture Agency: p. 116 (b); K. Ward: p. 123.

BIOS

Ch. Courteaup: 19 (b).

INSTITUT OCÉANOGRAPHIQUE, FONDATION ALBERT 1ER, PRINCE DE MONACO

Oceanographic Institute, Albert 1st, Prince of Monaco Foundation: p. 54 (b).

SHUTTERSTOCK, INC.

Altanak: p. 49.